Preface

In the ever-evolving landscape of computer science, the study of data structures and algorithms remains a cornerstone of both academic inquiry and practical application. This book, **"Data Structure and Algorithm Previous Year Question Book",** is a meticulously curated resource, designed to bridge the gap between theoretical knowledge and its implementation in real-world scenarios. As the complexity and scale of data-driven systems continue to grow, a profound understanding of these fundamental concepts is essential for any aspiring software engineer, researcher, or computer science professional.

The content of this book is structured to provide comprehensive coverage of the most critical topics in data structures and algorithms. Each chapter is crafted with precision, offering an in-depth exploration of concepts such as arrays, linked lists, stacks, queues, trees, graphs, and a wide variety of sorting and searching algorithms. The theoretical underpinnings are presented in a clear and concise manner, ensuring that the foundational principles are well understood before progressing to more complex topics.

A unique feature of this book is the integration of previous year exam questions, which have been selected to represent a diverse range of problem types and difficulty levels. Each question is accompanied by a detailed solution, meticulously crafted to guide the reader through the problem-solving process. These solutions not only provide the correct answers but also elucidate the underlying logic and algorithms, fostering a deeper comprehension of the material.

In recognition of the diverse learning preferences of readers, this book is complemented by a series of video tutorials. These tutorials serve as an extension of the written content, providing a visual and interactive medium for learning. By engaging with these resources, readers will be better equipped to tackle the challenges presented in both academic and professional settings.

We hope that this book serves as a valuable tool in your journey to mastering data structures and algorithms, and that it helps you build a robust foundation for future success in the field of computer science.

Table of Contents

MCS – 208

Post Graduate Diploma in Computer Applications (PGDCA)

Chapter 1: Term-End Examination, December, 2021

MCS-208: Data Structures and Algorithms

Time: 3 Hours

Maximum Marks: 100

Weightage: 70%

Note: Question No. 1 is compulsory. Attempt any three Questions from the rest.

1. (a)Define "Time Complexity" and "Space Complexity". What are the differences between them? 10

(b) Write an algorithm for bubble sort. Sort the following set of data in ascending order using bubble sort. Show all steps of application of algorithm: 100, 50, 60, 70, 150, 80 10

(c) Define "Stack". Explain the operations that can be performed on a stack. 10

(d) Write an algorithm to reverse a string. 10

2. (a)Write an algorithm to insert an element into a singly linked list. Make necessary assumptions. 10

(b) What is a Tree? How does it differ from a Binary Tree? 10

3. (a) Write Kruskal's algorithm. 10

(b) What is Binary Search? Explain it with an example. 10

4. (a)Write an algorithm for addition of two matrices. 10

(b) What is Depth First Search? Explain it with an example. 10

5. (a) What is a Circular Queue? How does it differ from a queue? 10

(b) Explain any two types of traversals of binary trees. 10

MCS – 208

Post Graduate Diploma in Computer Applications (PGDCA)

Chapter 2: Term-End Examination, June, 2022

MCS-208: Data Structures And Algorithms

Time: 3 Hours

Maximum Marks: 100

Weightage: 70%

Note: Question No. 1 is compulsory. Attempt any three Questions from the rest.

1. (a) What is meant by *Big-O* notation? Explain with an example. *10*

(b) Write an algorithm for Quick Sort. Sort the following set of data in ascending order using Quick Sort. Show all steps of application of algorithm: 110, 50, 60, 70, 150, 80 *10*

(c) Define ''Queue''. Explain the operations that can be performed on a Queue. *10*

(d) Write an algorithm that accepts two strings, S1 and S2, as input and then find whether S1 is a substring of S2. *10*

2. (a) Write an algorithm to delete an element from a Singly Linked List. Make necessary assumptions. *10*

(b) Explain the process of converting a Tree to a Binary Tree with an example. *10*

2. (a) What is meant by Minimum Cost Spanning Tree (MCST)? How can you find it? *10*

(b) What is Linear Search? How does it differ from Binary Search? *10*

2. (a) Write an algorithm for multiplication of two matrices. *10*

(b) What is Breadth-First Search? Explain it with an example. *10*

2. (a) What is a Dequeue? How does it differ from a Queue? *10*

(b) Write an algorithm for inorder traversal of a Binary Tree. *10*

MCS – 208

Post Graduate Diploma in Computer Applications (PGDCA)

Chapter 3: Term-End Examination, December, 2022

MCS-208: Data Structures and Algorithms

Time: 3 Hours

Maximum Marks: 100

Weightage: 70%

Note: Question No. 1 is compulsory. Answer any three Questions from the rest.

1. (a) Explain the operations that are performed on Stacks. Write an algorithm to push an element to the stack. *10*

(b) What are Arrays? Write an algorithm to multiply two matrices. *10*

(c) What is Binary Search? Write an algorithm for it. *10*

(d). Convert the following expression to postfix: (a + b) / (c – d) *10*

2. (a) What is a Stack? Write an algorithm for implementation of a Stack. *10*

3. What is Storage Complexity? How does it differ from Time Complexity? *10*

4. (a) What are Singly Linked Lists? Write an algorithm for implementation of a Singly Linked List. *10*

(b) What is a Binary Tree? How does it differ from a tree? Write an algorithm for traversal of a Binary Tree. *10*

5. (a) What are the properties of an AVL tree? Explain the possible rotations that are possible on an unbalanced AVL tree. *10*

(b) Write Dijkstra's algorithm. *10*

6. (a) What is Breadth First Search? How does it differ from Depth First Search? *10*

(b) What is Hashing? Write a short note on it. *10*

Chapter 4: Mostly Asked Important Questions – Part A

Q1. Define Time Complexity and Space Complexity. How do they differ?

Answer: Time complexity measures the amount of time an algorithm takes to execute as a function of input size, while space complexity measures the amount of memory used by the algorithm during execution. Time complexity focuses on speed, whereas space complexity focuses on memory requirements.

Q2. Write an algorithm for Quick Sort and explain its steps on a sample array.

Answer: Quick Sort is a divide-and-conquer algorithm that selects a pivot element, partitions the array into two subarrays, and recursively applies the same process. The steps involve choosing a pivot, rearranging elements such that all smaller elements are to the left and larger ones to the right, and applying the process to subarrays.

Q3. Explain Big-O notation with an example.

Answer: Big-O notation describes the upper bound of an algorithm's runtime, representing its worst-case time complexity. For example, linear search over an array of size nnn has a time complexity of O(n)O(n)O(n) because it may need to check each element once.

Q4. Define a Stack and explain its operations. Provide an algorithm to implement a stack using an array.

Answer: A stack is a linear data structure that follows the Last In First Out (LIFO) principle. The main operations are push (insert), pop (remove), and peek (view top element). To implement a stack with an array, use a variable top to track the index of the last inserted element.

Q5. Define a Queue. Explain how a circular queue works and how it differs from a linear queue.

Answer: A queue is a linear data structure that follows the First In First Out (FIFO) principle. A circular queue connects the end of the queue to its front, allowing efficient use of memory by reusing emptied array positions. In a linear queue, once the rear reaches the end of the array, no more insertions are possible even if there are empty spaces at the front.

Q6. What are circular linked lists? Provide an algorithm to insert an element into a circular linked list.

Answer: A circular linked list is a variation of a linked list where the last node points back to the first node. To insert a new node, create the node, adjust the last node's pointer to the new node, and set the new node's pointer to the head node.

Q7. What is a full tree? What is a complete tree? How can a binary tree be implemented using linked lists?

Answer: A full tree is a tree where every node has either zero or two children. A complete tree is a tree where all levels are completely filled except possibly the last level, which is filled from left to right. A binary tree can be implemented using linked lists by defining a node structure with data, a pointer to the left child, and a pointer to the right child.

Q8. Write Prim's algorithm to find the Minimum Cost Spanning Tree (MCST).

Answer: Prim's algorithm starts with a single vertex and grows the MCST by adding the smallest edge that connects a vertex in the tree to a vertex outside it, until all vertices are included.

Q9. Write Dijkstra's algorithm for finding the shortest path from a single source in a graph.

Answer: Dijkstra's algorithm initializes distances from the source to all vertices as infinity, except the source itself which is set to zero. It repeatedly selects the vertex with the smallest distance, updates the distances of its neighbors, and marks the vertex as visited until all vertices are processed.

Q10. Explain Depth First Search (DFS) and Breadth First Search (BFS) graph traversal techniques with examples.

Answer: DFS explores as deep as possible along each branch before backtracking and is implemented using a stack or recursion. BFS explores all neighbors at the current depth before moving to nodes at the next level and is implemented using a queue. Both algorithms can be illustrated by traversing a sample graph and showing the order of visited nodes.

Chapter 5: Mostly Asked Important Questions – Part B

Q1. Explain how dynamic memory allocation works in C/C++ and why it is important in implementing linked data structures like linked lists, trees, and graphs.

Answer: Dynamic memory allocation uses functions like malloc, calloc, realloc in C or new/delete in C++, allowing runtime allocation of memory. This flexibility is crucial for linked structures where the number of elements isn't known in advance. It enables efficient memory usage, avoids wastage from fixed-size static arrays, and supports dynamic growth and shrinkage of data structures at runtime.

Q2. Describe the process and advantages of implementing two stacks in a single array. Include pseudocode for push and pop operations.

Answer: Two stacks can share one array by growing from opposite ends (one from start, one from end). This saves space by using a single buffer and is efficient when the total number of stack elements is bounded. Pseudocode ensures top1 < top2 to avoid overflow. Push updates top1++ or top2--, and pop retrieves and adjusts the respective top.

Q3. Explain what a Trie (prefix tree) is, its typical use cases, and how insertion and search operations work.

Answer: A Trie is a tree-like structure used to store dynamic sets of strings, where each node represents a character. It's commonly used in prefix-based search, auto-complete, and dictionary implementations. To insert, you traverse the tree character by character, creating nodes if needed. To search, you follow the path of characters; presence of a marked terminal node indicates a valid string.

Q4. Discuss the trade-offs between using adjacency matrices and adjacency lists for graph representation, with respect to memory usage and algorithmic efficiency.

Answer: An adjacency matrix uses O(V2)O(V^2)O(V2) space but allows O(1)O(1)O(1) edge-existence checks—suitable for dense graphs. Adjacency lists use O(V+E)O(V + E)O(V+E) space and are efficient for sparse graphs. Iterating neighbors is O(degree(v))O(degree(v))O(degree(v)) vs scanning full row in a matrix. Choice depends on graph density and types of operations performed.

Q5. Describe the algorithm for deleting a node with a given value from a binary search tree (BST). Include handling for nodes with zero, one, or two children.

Answer:

- **Leaf node**: simply remove it.
- **Single child**: replace the node with its child.
- **Two children**: find in-order successor (minimum in right subtree), copy its value to the node, and recursively delete the successor, which will be a leaf or single-child node.

Q6. Explain the workings of merge sort and compare its performance with quick sort in average and worst-case scenarios.

Answer: Merge sort is a divide-and-conquer algorithm that splits the array into halves, recursively sorts them, and merges the sorted halves. It guarantees O(nlog n)O(n \log n)O(nlogn) time in both average and worst cases and uses O(n)O(n)O(n) auxiliary space. Quick sort has O(nlog n)O(n \log n)O(nlogn) average time but degrades to O(n2)O(n^2)O(n2) in worst-case (e.g., sorted input with poor pivot choice), although it can sort in-place with O(log n)O(\log n)O(logn) extra space on average.

Q7. Define a priority queue and explain how a binary heap implements it. Describe insertion and deletion steps.

Answer: A priority queue is an abstract data type where each element has a priority, and removal returns the highest (or lowest) priority item. A binary heap (max-heap or min-heap) is the typical implementation: a nearly complete binary tree represented as an array.

- **Insertion**: add new element at end, then "heapify-up" (swap with parent until heap property holds).
- **Deletion**: remove root, move last element to root, then "heapify-down" (swap with the larger child until heap property holds).

Q8. Explain the concept of hashing, hash functions, and collision resolution techniques like chaining and open addressing.

Answer: Hashing maps keys to an index in a fixed-size table using a hash function (e.g., modulo-based). Collisions occur when multiple keys map to the same index.

- **Chaining**: each bucket holds a list of entries.
- **Open addressing**: probes other indices (linear, quadratic, or double hashing). Efficiency depends on load factor; as it increases, performance declines.

Q9. Describe graph traversal using Topological Sort. When is it applicable, and how is it implemented?

Answer: Topological Sort orders the vertices of a Directed Acyclic Graph (DAG) such that for every directed edge u→vu \to vu→v, uuu precedes vvv. It's used in scheduling tasks with dependencies. Implementations include Kahn's algorithm (remove nodes with zero in-degree iteratively) or DFS-based method (perform DFS, pushing nodes onto a stack upon recursion return).

Q10. Explain the concept of amortized analysis with an example, such as dynamic array resizing.

Answer: Amortized analysis evaluates the average cost per operation over a sequence of operations, smoothing worst-case spikes. For dynamic array resizing: appending is usually O(1)O(1)O(1), but when the array doubles, resizing is O(n)O(n)O(n). Spread over many appends, the average cost remains O(1)O(1)O(1) per operation.

Chapter 6: Mostly Asked Important Questions – Part C

Q1. Explain in detail how merge sort works. Provide the algorithm steps, explain the divide-and-conquer strategy, and discuss time and space complexity along with practical scenarios where merge sort is preferred.

Answer: Merge sort recursively divides the array into halves until single-element arrays are reached. In the conquer phase, it merges adjacent sorted subarrays into larger sorted arrays. The time complexity is O(nlog n)O(n \log n)O(nlogn) in all cases, and space complexity is O(n)O(n)O(n) due to auxiliary arrays. Merge sort is preferred for stable sorting and handling large datasets in external memory where random access is expensive.

Q2. Describe how to implement an LRU (Least Recently Used) cache with O(1) access, insertion, and deletion. Explain the data structures used and how they operate together.

Answer: An LRU cache combines a HashMap and a doubly linked list. The HashMap provides O(1) look-up for keys. The doubly linked list maintains usage order so the least recently used item is at the tail. On access or insertion, if the key exists, move its node to the head. If inserting a new key when full, remove the tail node, delete it from the map, then insert the new node at the head and update the map.

Q3. Explain Dijkstra's algorithm in detail, including how it handles weighted graphs, uses priority queues, and why it fails with negative edge weights. Provide pseudocode.

Answer: Dijkstra's algorithm finds shortest paths from a source node in a graph with non-negative edge weights. It uses a priority queue to select the unvisited node with the smallest known distance and updates the distances of its neighbors if a shorter path is found. It fails with negative edge weights because once a node is visited, its distance is considered final, but negative weights could later provide a shorter path, violating this assumption.

Q4. Compare and contrast quick sort and heap sort. Discuss performance, memory usage, stability, and typical use cases for each algorithm.

Answer: Quick sort has O(nlog n)O(n \log n)O(nlogn) average time complexity but O(n2)O(n^2)O(n2) in the worst case, uses O(log n)O(\log n)O(logn) space, and is not stable. Heap sort has guaranteed O(nlog n)O(n \log n)O(nlogn) performance, uses O(1) extra space, and is also not stable. Quick sort is faster on average and better for in-memory sorting, while heap sort is chosen when worst-case performance guarantees are required.

Q5. Explain how a red-black tree maintains balance. Describe its properties, insertion and deletion operations, and the role of color flipping and rotations.

Answer: A red-black tree is a self-balancing binary search tree. Its properties ensure balance: each node is red or black, the root is black, red nodes cannot have red children, and every path from root to leaves has the same number of black nodes. Insertions and deletions may cause violations of these properties and are fixed using rotations and color flips to rebalance the tree while maintaining O(log n)O(\log n)O(logn) height.

Q6. Describe the union-find (disjoint set) data structure. Explain how union by rank and path compression optimize operations, and provide their time complexity.

Answer: Union-find manages disjoint sets with operations `find(x)` to identify the root and `union(x, y)` to merge sets. Union by rank attaches the smaller tree under the larger tree to keep the tree shallow. Path compression flattens the tree during find operations, pointing every node directly to the root. These optimizations give nearly constant time performance, with amortized time complexity of O(α(n))O(\alpha(n))O(α(n)), where α\alphaα is the inverse Ackermann function.

Q7. Explain in detail how breadth-first search (BFS) can be used to find the shortest path in an unweighted graph. Include pseudocode.

Answer: BFS starts at the source node, visiting all neighbors first, then neighbors of neighbors, using a queue to track nodes. To find the shortest path, each time a neighbor is added to the queue, record its parent. When the destination is found, backtrack using parent pointers to reconstruct the path. BFS guarantees the shortest path in terms of the number of edges because it explores nodes level by level.

Q8. Compare chaining vs open addressing in hash tables by analyzing load factor thresholds, memory overhead, and cache performance. When is one preferred over the other?

Answer: Chaining stores multiple items at each bucket using linked lists and tolerates load factors greater than 1. It has higher memory overhead due to pointers but performs well under high load. Open addressing stores items directly in the array and resolves collisions via probing. It requires the load factor to stay below ~0.7 to prevent clustering but has better cache performance due to contiguous memory. Chaining is preferred for dynamic resizing, while open addressing is favored when memory locality is critical.

Q9. Describe Tarjan's algorithm for finding strongly connected components (SCC) in a directed graph. Explain how stack usage and DFS timestamps help identify SCCs.

Answer: Tarjan's algorithm performs a DFS, assigning each node an index and a lowlink value (the smallest index reachable). Nodes are pushed onto a stack as they are visited. When a node's index equals its lowlink value, all nodes on the stack above it form a strongly connected component. These nodes are popped off the stack together. This process identifies SCCs efficiently in O(V+E)O(V+E)O(V+E) time.

Q10. Explain what amortized analysis is and work through an example of insertions in a dynamically resizing array (e.g., doubling strategy). Calculate the average cost per insertion over n insertions.

Answer: Amortized analysis spreads the cost of expensive operations over many cheap ones to compute an average cost per operation. For dynamic arrays that double in size, most insertions are O(1)O(1)O(1) except when resizing occurs, which takes O(n)O(n)O(n). Across nnn insertions, total resizing cost is O(n)O(n)O(n), so the average amortized cost per insertion remains O(1)O(1)O(1).

Chapter 7: Mostly Asked Important Questions – Part D

Q1. Explain how the Floyd–Warshall algorithm computes shortest paths in a weighted graph. Include time and space complexity, and scenarios where it is preferred over Dijkstra's algorithm.

Answer: Floyd–Warshall is a dynamic programming algorithm that computes shortest paths between every pair of vertices in O(V3)O(V^3)O(V3) time and uses O(V2)O(V^2)O(V2) space for its distance matrix. It iteratively updates distances by checking if going through each intermediate node yields shorter paths. It handles negative edge weights (but not negative cycles) and is preferred when all-pairs shortest paths are required, especially in dense graphs or smaller networks.

Q2. Describe the design and implementation of a Bloom filter. How does it trade accuracy for space efficiency?

Answer: A Bloom filter is a probabilistic data structure using a bit array and multiple hash functions. Insertion sets bits at hash-determined positions; lookup checks all positions. It can have false positives but no false negatives. Its space efficiency stems from needing only O(m)O(m)O(m) bits for nnn items and a low false-positive rate, making it suitable for memory-constrained applications like web caches or network routers.

Q3. Explain the concept of the suffix tree and its application in substring search. What is its construction algorithm and complexity?

Answer: A suffix tree is a compressed trie of all suffixes of a string, enabling substring searches in O(m)O(m)O(m) time where mmm is the pattern length. Ukkonen's algorithm builds the suffix tree in O(n)O(n)O(n) time and O(n)O(n)O(n) space. Applications include pattern search, longest repeated substring detection, and genome assembly.

Q4. How does the A search algorithm find the shortest path, and how do admissible heuristics affect its performance? Provide an example.*

Answer: A* search uses priority-ordered exploration with f(n)=g(n)+h(n)f(n) = g(n) + h(n)f(n)=g(n)+h(n), where g(n)g(n)g(n) is the cost from the start and h(n)h(n)h(n) is a heuristic estimate of the remaining cost. An admissible heuristic never overestimates the actual cost, ensuring an optimal path. For instance, using Euclidean distance in a grid ensures both correctness and better performance.

Q5. Explain the concept of red–black tree deletion in detail. How does it differ from insertion, and what cases must be handled during deletion rebalancing?

Answer: Red–black tree deletion begins by removing the target node or replacing it with its successor. After removing, a "double black" violation might occur. The algorithm addresses six cases involving sibling color and children color, using rotations and recoloring to restore tree properties. Deletion is generally more complex than insertion due to these multiple rebalancing scenarios.

Q6. Describe the concept of Fibonacci heaps. What operations do they optimize, and what are the amortized complexities?

Answer: Fibonacci heaps are advanced heap structures that support insert, find-min, and decrease-key in O(1)O(1)O(1) amortized time, and delete-min in O(log n)O(\log n)O(logn). They use a collection of trees with lazy merging and cascading cuts. They are particularly useful in graph algorithms (e.g., Dijkstra, MST) that perform many decrease-key operations.

Q7. Compare linear probing, quadratic probing, and double hashing in open addressing. Discuss advantages and typical probe counts under different load factors.

Answer: Linear probing increments linearly on collision, leading to primary clustering but simplicity. Quadratic probing jumps quadratically, reducing clustering but risking cycles. Double hashing uses a second hash for step size, offering better distribution and lowest clustering. Under load factors <0.7, linear and quadratic perform well; double hashing handles higher loads more gracefully.

Q8. Explain how the suffix array and LCP (Longest Common Prefix) array are built and how they enable fast substring searching. Include construction complexity.

Answer: A suffix array lists all suffixes of a string in lexicographic order. It can be built in O(nlog n)O(n \log n)O(nlogn) using suffix doubling or in O(n)O(n)O(n) with advanced algorithms. The LCP array stores the longest common prefixes between adjacent suffixes, enabling binary search to perform substring matching in O(mlog n)O(m \log n)O(mlogn), where mmm is the pattern length.

Q9. Describe Kosaraju's algorithm for finding strongly connected components (SCC) in directed graphs. Compare its approach and complexity to Tarjan's algorithm.

Answer: Kosaraju's algorithm performs two DFS traversals in O(V+E)O(V+E)O(V+E): first to fill a stack in order of completion times, then DFS on the transposed graph in stack order to discover SCCs. Tarjan's algorithm finds SCCs in one DFS using lowlink and a stack. Tarjan is more efficient in practice (one pass), but Kosaraju's is simpler to implement conceptually.

Q10. Explain the concept and implementation of segment trees with lazy propagation. When are they used, and how does lazy update work?

Answer: Segment trees allow efficient range queries and updates in O(log n)O(\log n)O(logn). With lazy propagation, range updates are deferred by storing pending update values in internal nodes. When a query reaches a node with a pending update, the update is applied and propagated to children only when needed. This avoids unnecessary recomputation and supports fast, multi-update operations.

Chapter 8: Mostly Asked Important Questions – Part E

Q1. Explain the concept of the "minimum cut" in a flow network. Describe the Max-Flow Min-Cut theorem and outline the Ford–Fulkerson method for computing maximum flow.

Answer: A minimum cut in a flow network partitions the nodes into two sets (source side and sink side) such that the total capacity of edges crossing from the source set to the sink set is minimized. The Max-Flow Min-Cut theorem states that the maximum amount of flow that can pass from source to sink equals the capacity of the minimum cut. Ford–Fulkerson iteratively finds augmenting paths from source to sink in the residual graph and updates flows until no augmenting path exists. The result is a maximum flow and corresponding minimum cut.

Q2. Describe the B-tree data structure. Explain how insertion, deletion, and search operations work, and why B-trees are widely used in database indexing and file systems.

Answer: A B-tree is a self-balancing, multi-way search tree designed for systems that read and write large blocks of data. Each node can have multiple keys and children. Insertion places the key in a leaf node and splits the node if it overflows; deletion may require merging or borrowing from siblings to maintain minimum occupancy. Searching is done by traversing downward through key intervals. B-trees minimize disk I/O and maintain logarithmic operation times, making them ideal for databases and filesystems.

Q3. Explain the concept of "skip lists." How do they achieve average-case O(log n) search, insertion, and deletion, and how do they compare to balanced trees?

Answer: Skip lists are probabilistic data structures that maintain multiple layers of linked lists, where higher layers skip over multiple elements in lower layers. Each element is promoted to higher layers based on coin flips, typically with a 50% chance. Search, insertion, and deletion begin at the highest level and move down upon overshoot, resulting in an expected O(log n) time complexity. Skip lists match balanced trees in performance and are simpler to implement and randomized.

Q4. What is the "k-d tree"? Explain how it supports efficient nearest-neighbor searches in multidimensional space.

Answer: A k-d tree is a space-partitioning structure for organizing points in k-dimensional space. It alternates splitting dimensions at each level, partitioning the region into hyperrectangles. Nearest-neighbor search traverses the tree recursively, pruning branches that cannot contain closer points based on distance to the splitting hyperplane. Average search time is O(log n), but worst-case can be O(n). It's commonly used in spatial indexing and computer graphics.

Q5. Describe the concept of "graph coloring." Explain how the greedy coloring algorithm works and where graph coloring is applied.

Answer: Graph coloring assigns colors to vertices so that no two adjacent vertices share the same color. The greedy algorithm iterates vertices in a sequence, assigning the smallest available color not used by its neighbors. While simple and fast (O(V + E)), it doesn't always yield an optimal coloring. Graph coloring is used in applications like register allocation in compilers, scheduling problems, and frequency assignment in networks.

Q6. Explain the concept of a "trie with compressed paths" (also known as a Patricia trie). How does it improve storage efficiency, and where is it useful?

Answer: A Patricia trie compresses chains of single-child nodes into one edge labeled with the concatenated path. This reduces memory usage and speeds up searches by skipping multiple nodes. It stores key–value pairs compactly, making it ideal for applications like routers, IP address management, and prefix matching where path compression yields significant space savings.

Q7. Describe the concept of "k-means clustering" as an algorithmic process. How does it relate to Voronoi diagrams and what are its main limitations?

Answer: K-means clustering partitions a set of points into k clusters by repeating two steps: assigning each point to the nearest centroid, and then recomputing centroids as the mean of assigned points. This continues until centroids stabilize. It relates to Voronoi diagrams, as each cluster forms a Voronoi cell around its centroid. Limitations include sensitivity to initial centroid placement and convergence to local optima, making results non-deterministic unless careful initialization is used.

Q8. Explain the concept of "persistent data structures." Provide an example of how a persistent linked list allows access to past versions.

Answer: Persistent data structures allow access to previous versions after updates without modifying them. In a persistent linked list, inserting an element at the head creates a new node pointing to the old head. The previous head remains intact, preserving the older version. This enables structural sharing and efficient version control, useful in functional programming, undo systems, and concurrent data access.

Q9. What are "skip-graphs"? Explain how they extend skip lists for efficient range queries in distributed systems.

Answer: Skip-graphs are a peer-to-peer indexing structure that generalizes skip lists across multiple dimensions or nodes. They form sorted lists on various levels distributed among peers and connect nodes with shared prefixes. Skip-graphs support efficient range queries and dynamic membership, making them useful in P2P networks for scalable indexing and lookup.

Q10. Describe "online algorithms" versus "offline algorithms." Provide an example of an online algorithm in data structures and explain how its performance is measured.

Answer: Online algorithms process input piece-by-piece without knowledge of future inputs. Offline algorithms have full access to all input beforehand. An example is the list update problem managed by Move-to-Front heuristic, where access operations dynamically adjust the list. Performance is measured via competitive analysis, comparing the online algorithm's performance with the optimal offline counterpart. For Move-to-Front, it guarantees competitiveness close to 2.

Chapter 9: Mostly Asked Important Questions – Part F

Q1. Explain the concept of "minimax algorithm" with alpha-beta pruning in game trees. Describe how pruning improves efficiency and provide the conditions for pruning.

Answer: The minimax algorithm explores all possible game states to a certain depth, assuming two players alternate maximizing and minimizing a score. Alpha-beta pruning eliminates branches that cannot influence the final decision:

Alpha is the best already explored option along the path to the maximizer,

Beta is the best already explored option along the path to the minimizer.

When alpha ≥ beta, further exploration can be pruned. This reduces effective branching factor, significantly improving efficiency.

Q2. What is a "heavy-light decomposition"? Explain how it is used to optimize path queries on trees.

Answer: Heavy-light decomposition partitions a tree into "heavy" paths where children with the largest subtrees are linked, and "light" edges elsewhere. This transforms tree path queries into segment-tree or Fenwick-tree operations on heavy paths. Each query or update can be broken into $O(\log^2 n)$ segments, enabling efficient processing of path sums or updates.

Q3. Describe the concept of "range minimum query (RMQ)" and its O(1) solution using sparse tables.

Answer: RMQ answers the minimum value in a range [L, R] of a static array. Using a sparse table, we precompute minimums for intervals of lengths that are powers of two. Each query can then be answered in O(1) time by combining two overlapping intervals:

```
min(A[L, L+2^k-1], A[R-2^k+1, R]).
```

Q4. Explain the concept of "skip quadtree" and how it enhances multidimensional range queries.

Answer: A skip quadtree layers quadtrees of decreasing powers-of-two grid resolution—larger spatial regions at higher levels, more detail at lower levels. It allows efficient spatial queries (like range search or nearest neighbor) by traversing coarsest to finest layers, pruning entire regions when possible, and reducing complexity in 2D search contexts.

Q5. What is an "interval tree"? Describe how it handles interval overlap queries and give an outline of its implementation using an augmented BST.

Answer: An interval tree stores intervals in a balanced BST keyed by their start values. Each node is augmented with the maximum end value of its subtree. To query overlaps with [L, R], starting at the root, compare intervals and skip subtrees whose max-end is less than L. This supports insertion, deletion, and overlap search in O(log n) time.

Q6. Explain the concept of "orthogonal range searching" using k-d trees or range trees. How does it perform in multidimensional data?

Answer: Orthogonal range searching retrieves all points within a hyper-rectangular query region.

- With **k-d trees**, space is recursively partitioned by alternating dimensions—range queries traverse only branches overlapping the region, taking O(log n + k) time (k = results).

- With **range trees**, a BST on one axis is augmented with secondary trees on the other axis, yielding $O(\log^2 n + k)$ time and O(n log n) space, suitable when multidimensional indexing is needed.

Q7. Describe the "Suffix Automaton" data structure. What problems does it solve efficiently and what is its construction complexity?

Answer: A suffix automaton is a minimal DFA accepting all substrings of a string. It supports efficient substring, distinct substring count, and longest common substring queries. It is built in O(n) time and space by extending the automaton with each character and updating states and transitions. This automaton is more compact than suffix trees for many string-processing tasks.

Q8. Explain the "Dynamic Tree" (Link-Cut tree). How does it enable operations like link, cut, and path queries in O(log n) time?

Answer: A link-cut tree represents a forest using splay trees to maintain paths.

- **link(u, v)** connects two trees,
- **cut(u)** detaches a subtree,
- Path queries like sum or max along the root path are supported.

Splay tree rotations ensure each operation takes amortized O(log n) time.

Q9. What is a "compressed bitmap index"? Explain how bit-level compression (like run-length encoding or word-aligned hybrid) supports fast bitwise operations.

Answer: A compressed bitmap uses compression—e.g., run-length encoding or word-aligned hybrid to store bitmaps compactly when data has long runs of 0s or 1s. Logical operations (AND, OR) can be performed on compressed segments without decompressing, enabling fast set operations and efficient storage for sparse or dense boolean datasets.

Q10. Describe the concept of "approximate nearest neighbor (ANN)" using locality-sensitive hashing (LSH). How does it reduce search complexity in high-dimensional spaces?

Answer: LSH hashes vectors into buckets such that similar items are likely to fall into the same bucket, using random projections suitable for specific metrics (e.g., cosine, Euclidean). During search, the query is hashed and neighbors are retrieved from candidate buckets. This approximate search runs in sublinear time (e.g., O(n^ρ)) in high dimensions, and is widely used in image recognition and recommendation systems.

Chapter 10: Mostly Asked Important Questions – Part G

Q1. Describe the concept of "persistent segment trees." How do they differ from standard segment trees, and how are updates handled to preserve previous versions?

Answer: A persistent segment tree allows access to all previous versions after updates. Instead of modifying nodes in place, it clones only the nodes along the update path, preserving unmodified subtrees by sharing them. Each update produces a new root, with updates taking O(log n)O(\log n)O(logn) time and space. This enables versioning and retrospective queries without rebuilding the structure.

Q2. Explain the "suffix automaton" concept more deeply with an example. How can it be used to count distinct substrings in a string efficiently?

Answer: A suffix automaton is a minimal deterministic finite automaton recognizing all substrings. Each state represents end positions of substrings. To count distinct substrings, compute the sum across all states of (len[state] – len[link[state]]), where len is the state's length and link points to its suffix link. This runs in linear time, i.e., O(n)O(n)O(n).

Q3. What are "wavelet trees," and how are they used to support queries like kth-order statistics and rank/select on compressed strings?

Answer: A wavelet tree is a binary tree built over an alphabet that recursively recursively partitions characters. It supports operations such as access, rank (count occurrences up to an index), and select (find the position of the kth occurrence) in O(log |Σ|)O(\log |\Sigma|)O(log|Σ|) per query. It's efficient for compressed text processing with high query speed and low memory footprint.

Q4. Describe the concept of "efficient dynamic connectivity" using Union-Find with rollback. How is the structure modified to support undo operations?

Answer: To support undo operations, Union-Find is augmented to store history stacks of parent and rank changes for each union. Rollback restores the previous state by reversing stack updates. Each union records what changed, enabling backtracking in O(1)O(1)O(1) per rollback. This is vital in offline dynamic connectivity applications, such as evolving graphs over time.

Q5. Explain the concept of "kth smallest number in a sliding window" using a dual-heap approach. How does it maintain balance between two heaps?

Answer: Maintain two heaps (max-heap for lower half, min-heap for upper half). When sliding the window, insert new value in one heap, remove expired value from the appropriate heap, and rebalance sizes to differ by at most 1. The root of one heap gives the kth smallest. Insertion, deletion, and rebalancing each take O(log k)O(\log k)O(logk) time.

Q6. What is a "range add, range sum query" segment tree with lazy propagation? How is it implemented and updated efficiently?

Answer: This segment tree supports adding a value to all elements within a range and querying the sum of a range. It stores lazy "add" values in nodes. During update, it adjusts the node's sum and propagates lazy tags to children only when needed (on push-down). Both updates and queries take O(log n)O(\log n)O(logn) time with lazy propagation.

Q7. Describe the "Euler Tour Tree" structure. How can it dynamically support subtree and path queries in an evolving tree?

Answer: An Euler tour tree linearizes a rooted tree by its Euler tour sequence, stored in a balanced BST or Fenwick tree. Subtree queries become contiguous segment queries over the tour sequence, and path queries can be decomposed similarly. The structure supports dynamic link/cut tree updates via splitting/concatenating the tour in O(log n)O(\log n)O(logn).

Q8. Explain "lowest common ancestor (LCA)" computation via binary lifting. How is the preprocessing done and how are queries answered in O(log n)O(\log n)O(logn)?

Answer: Preprocessing stores up[v][k], the 2^k–th ancestor of node v, for each v and k in a DP table. Also store depth of nodes. For each query (u, v), lift the deeper node to the same depth, then simultaneously lift both up until they meet. Each lift uses binary jumps, so queries are answered in O(log n)O(\log n)O(logn) time and preprocessing takes O(nlog n)O(n \log n)O(nlogn).

Q9. Describe the concept of "range XOR queries" using segment trees. How does the unbiased bitwise nature of XOR change the tree implementation?

Answer: Since XOR is associative and its own inverse, lazy propagation is simpler—updates only need to keep a lazy XOR value. A node's value is XORed with the lazy tag multiplied appropriately (based on segment length). Propagation to children XORs their tags. Range XOR queries and updates are implemented in O(log n)O(\log n)O(logn) time.

Q10. Explain how "convolution" can be computed using Fast Fourier Transform (FFT) and describe an application in polynomial multiplication.

Answer: FFT multiplies two polynomials by evaluating them at the nth roots of unity, point-wise multiplying evaluations, and using inverse FFT to reconstruct coefficients. It reduces polynomial multiplication from naive O(n2)O(n^2)O(n2) to O(nlog n)O(n \log n)O(nlogn), enabling efficient large integer arithmetic and signal processing applications.

Chapter 11: Mostly Asked Important Questions – Part H

Q1. Explain the concept of "top-k frequent elements" using a min-heap approach. How do you maintain the heap, and what is the time complexity?

Answer: Maintain a min-heap of size k containing the current top-k elements by frequency. Iterate over the frequency map; for each entry, insert into the heap if it's size < k or if the frequency is higher than the heap's root, replacing the root. Each insertion/pop is O(log k)O(\log k)O(logk), so overall time is O(nlog k)O(n \log k)O(nlogk).

Q2. Describe the algorithm for "range mutability" using a Fenwick Tree (Binary Indexed Tree) that supports both prefix sum and prefix update.

Answer: Use two BITs, BIT1 and BIT2. For range add [l, r], update BIT1 with +val at l and -val at r+1; update BIT2 with val*(l-1) at l and -val*r at r+1. The prefix-sum query at x is sum(BIT1, x)*x - sum(BIT2, x). Each operation is O(log n)O(\log n)O(logn).

Q3. What is the algorithm for finding the "longest increasing subsequence" (LIS) in O(nlog n)O(n \log n)O(nlogn) time? Describe the use of patience sorting and binary search.

Answer: Maintain an array tail[] where tail[i] is the smallest value that an increasing subsequence of length i+1 can end with. For each element, binary search in tail and replace/increment it accordingly. This yields the LIS length in O(nlog n)O(n \log n)O(nlogn).

Q4. Explain "range minimum XOR query" using a segment tree. How do you handle XOR instead of sum or minimum?

Answer: Build a segment tree that stores the XOR of elements for each range. For a query, traverse the tree exactly like sum queries, combining XOR results. Since XOR is associative, no lazy propagation is needed for point updates and queries, and operations run in O(log n)O(\log n)O(logn).

Q5. Describe algorithmic steps for "matrix exponentiation" using divide-and-conquer to compute large powers in O(k3log n)O(k^3 \log n)O(k3logn), where k is matrix dimension.

Answer: Use fast exponentiation: to compute AnA^nAn, if n is even compute half = A^(n/2) recursively, then return half * half; if odd, return A * A^(n-1). Each multiplication costs O(k3)O(k^3)O(k3), and there are O(log n)O(\log n)O(logn) multiplications, giving O(k3log n)O(k^3 \log n)O(k3logn).

Q6. Explain solving "2-SAT" problems in linear time using strongly connected components on implication graphs.

Answer: For each clause (u V v), add implications (¬u → v) and (¬v → u) to a directed graph. Compute SCCs. The 2-SAT instance is satisfiable if no variable and its negation are in the same SCC. Use Kosaraju or Tarjan in O(V+E)O(V + E)O(V+E).

Q7. Describe how "succinct data structures" like bit-vector with rank support fast bit queries in compressed memory.

Answer: Store a bit-vector in blocks with precomputed partial sums (superblocks and subblocks). The rank(i) query — number of 1s up to index i — is computed using precomputed block sums and a popcount on a partial block. This achieves O(1)O(1)O(1) query time with near-minimal space (n+o(n)n + o(n)n+o(n) bits).

Q8. Explain "dynamic tree connectivity" using Euler Tour Trees. How can edge insertion and deletion be supported in O(log n)O(\log n)O(logn) amortized time?

Answer: Represent the tree by its Euler tour in a balanced BST. To link two trees, splice the tours; to cut an edge, split the tour. BST splitting and merging each cost O(log n)O(\log n)O(logn). The BST maintains subtree connectivity implicitly, supporting connectivity queries and updates efficiently.

Q9. What is the "range GCD query" and how can it be answered in O(1)O(1)O(1) using a sparse table?

Answer: Precompute a sparse table st[k][i] storing GCD of range [i, i + 2^k - 1]. To answer query [L, R], compute len = floor(log2(R-L+1)), and return gcd(st[len][L], st[len][R - 2^len + 1]). Each query runs in O(1)O(1)O(1).

Q10. Explain "capacity scaling" in max-flow algorithms like Edmonds-Karp or Dinic. How does scaling improve performance?

Answer: Capacity scaling processes augmenting paths by finding flows above a threshold that halves each phase. Start with Δ\DeltaΔ as the highest power of two ≤ max capacity, then only use paths with residual capacities ≥ Δ\DeltaΔ. After exhausting paths, halve Δ\DeltaΔ, and repeat. This ensures O(E2log U)O(E^2 \log U)O(E2logU) complexity where UUU is the maximum capacity, improving over naive O(E2V)O(E^2 V)O(E2V).

Chapter 12: Mostly Asked Important Questions – Part I

Q1. What is a "Treap" data structure?

Answer: A treap is a randomized balanced binary search tree where each node has a key (for BST ordering) and a randomly assigned priority (for heap property). It maintains BST property on keys and max-heap or min-heap property on priorities. Insertions and deletions involve standard BST operations followed by rotations to restore heap property, giving expected O(log n)O(\log n)O(logn) time per operation.

Q2. Explain how "bitwise tricks" optimize certain data structure operations, such as using lowbit(x) for Fenwick Tree updates.

Answer: lowbit(x) returns the largest power of two dividing x (i.e., x & -x). It's used in Fenwick (BIT) tree updates to determine which parent nodes to update efficiently. This bit-level shortcut makes both update and query functions run in O(log n)O(\log n)O(logn) time.

Q3. Describe the "Conveyor Belt model" for BFS using a deque. In what scenarios is it useful?

Answer: This BFS variant uses a deque to process 0-1 weighted graphs where edges have weights 0 or 1. Neighbors reached via 0-weight edges are pushed to the front, while those via 1-weight edges go to the back. This ensures shortest-path distances in O(V+E)O(V + E)O(V+E) since it behaves like a 0-1 BFS without a priority queue.

Q4. What is the "Morris traversal" algorithm for binary trees?

Answer: Morris traversal performs in-order (or preorder) traversal with O(1)O(1)O(1) extra space by temporarily modifying pointers. It threads the tree—after visiting a node's left subtree, it creates a link from the rightmost node to the current node, then restores the tree as it goes. This avoids recursion or auxiliary stack.

Q5. Explain "Fenwick Tree vs Segment Tree" differences in functionality and use cases.

Answer: Fenwick Tree (BIT) supports point updates and prefix queries efficiently using bitwise operations, ideal for prefix sums. Segment Tree supports more versatile operations like range updates, range queries, and lazy propagation. Fenwick Tree is simpler and faster for simple tasks; Segment Tree is more flexible for complex range operations.

Q6. Describe the algorithm for "finding the kth largest element in an unsorted array" using Quickselect. What is its average and worst-case time complexity?

Answer: Quickselect partitions the array around a pivot and recursively searches in the relevant partition. On average, it runs in O(n)O(n)O(n). However, worst-case (e.g., poor pivot selections) it degrades to O(n2)O(n^2)O(n2). Using median-of-medians pivot selection can guarantee O(n)O(n)O(n) worst-case time.

Q7. What is a "Scapegoat Tree"? How does it maintain balance without node rotations?

Answer: A scapegoat tree is a self-balancing BST that tracks subtree sizes. When an insertion causes depth bounds to be exceeded, it identifies an ancestor ("scapegoat") whose subtree is overweight and rebuilds that subtree into a balanced BST. It guarantees amortized O(log n)O(\log n)O(logn) per operation without per-operation rotations.

Q8. Explain "order-statistic tree (augmented RB-tree)" and how it supports finding the kth smallest element.

Answer: An order-statistic tree augments each node with the size of its subtree. To find the kth smallest, we compare k with the size of the left subtree plus one; traverse left, return current, or traverse right with adjusted k accordingly. Each query runs in O(log n)O(\log n)O(logn).

Q9. What is the "bitset" data structure and how does it accelerate operations like intersection and union?

Answer: A bitset stores boolean values as bits in a word or array. Bitwise operations like AND (intersection) and OR (union) can process 64 or 128 bits at once, making operations extremely fast compared to iterating and checking each element individually. Bitsets are efficient when the domain size is fixed and dense.

Q10. Describe "Online bipartite matching" using the Kuhn–Munkres (Hungarian) algorithm. What is its time complexity?

Answer: The Hungarian algorithm finds maximum-weight (or perfect) matching in bipartite graphs. It constructs feasible labelings and repeatedly augments matchings using alternating paths, adjusting labels along the way. Its time complexity is O(n3)O(n^3)O(n3), but it reliably finds max-weight matchings and is used in tasks like assignment and scheduling.

Chapter 13: Mostly Asked Important Questions – Part J

Q1. What is a "Cartesian tree"? Describe its construction from an array and its typical uses in range queries or RMQ (Range Minimum Query).

Answer: A Cartesian tree is a binary tree derived from a sequence, where the in-order traversal reproduces the original sequence and the heap property applies to the values (e.g., parent ≤ children for RMQ). It can be constructed in O(n)O(n)O(n) using a stack to maintain ancestors. Cartesian trees allow RMQ reduction to LCA (Lowest Common Ancestor) problems and support efficient RMQ queries over static arrays.

Q2. Explain the "Boyer–Moore majority vote" algorithm for finding the majority element in a stream. What is its time and space complexity?

Answer: The Boyer–Moore algorithm maintains a candidate majority and a counter. For each element, if the counter is 0, set the current element as candidate; otherwise, increment or decrement the counter depending on a match. After one pass, the candidate is the majority if it appears more than n/2 times. It runs in O(n)O(n)O(n) time and O(1)O(1)O(1) space.

Q3. Describe the "Union-Find with weighted union" optimization (without path compression). How does it improve on naive union-find?

Answer: Weighted union always attaches the smaller tree under the larger tree based on size (or rank). This ensures trees remain shallower, improving the find operation time. With this optimization alone, the worst-case time per operation is O(log n)O(\log n)O(logn), better than the naive O(n)O(n)O(n).

Q4. What is the "KMP (Knuth–Morris–Pratt)" algorithm? Explain how its failure function (prefix function) is built and how it enables fast substring search.

Answer: KMP builds a failure (prefix) function that computes the longest prefix ending at each position that is also a suffix. This allows the search to skip re-examining characters upon mismatches, achieving O(n+m)O(n + m)O(n+m) time for pattern length m and text length n, with O(m)O(m)O(m) preprocessing time and space.

Q5. Describe the "Disjoint Sparse Table" and how it's used for immutable range queries like GCD or min.

Answer: A Disjoint Sparse Table stores answers for ranges aligned to powers of two, built in O(nlog n)O(n \log n)O(nlogn). Any query can be answered in O(1)O(1)O(1) by combining two precomputed entries without overlapping. It's efficient for immutable data where repeated queries are frequent.

Q6. Explain the "Dynamic Segment Tree" concept. How does it support sparse updates over a large range (e.g., 0 ≤ index < 10^18)?

Answer: A Dynamic Segment Tree uses pointers (or maps) to only allocate nodes for accessed segments lazily. This allows handling extremely large index ranges while consuming memory proportional only to the number of updates, not the range size. Each update and query still runs in O(log R)O(\log R)O(logR), where R is the range size.

Q7. What is the "Heavy Path Decomposition" technique? Describe how it optimizes tree path operations like path sum or path max.

Answer: Heavy Path Decomposition splits a tree into chains (heavy paths) and light edges. Operations on paths between two nodes are broken into O(log n) segments along heavy paths, each manipulated via segment trees or Fenwick Trees, enabling efficient path queries/updates in O(log 2n)O(\log^2 n)O(log2n).

Q8. Describe the concept of "Binary Indexed Tree of Vectors" (BIT with per-index containers). How can it support "range of vectors" queries like reporting k-th smallest in prefix?

Answer: Each BIT node contains a sorted vector (or multiset) of values updated in that range. For "k-th smallest in range [1..i]" queries, merge data from O(log n) nodes and binary search across the merged virtual structure. Each query/update takes O(log 2n)O(\log^2 n)O(log2n).

Q9. Explain the "Suffix Automaton construction" in terms of transitions and suffix links. How does it compress substring representation compared to suffix trees?

Answer: The suffix automaton clone and extend process maintains transitions on characters and suffix links. Each new character either extends existing states or creates a clone. It has linear-time construction and fewer states than suffix trees, making it memory-efficient while supporting substring operations in O(1)O(1)O(1) per character.

Q10. What is a "Cuckoo Hashing" scheme? Describe how insertions and rehashing are handled, and discuss its worst-case lookup time and average insertion time.

Answer: Cuckoo Hashing uses two (or more) hash functions and positions. Insertion tries one position; if occupied, evicts the existing element (kicked item), which is reinserted using its alternate position, continuing until place found or cycle detected. Lookup is O(1)O(1)O(1) worst-case (two checks), insertion is O(1)O(1)O(1) amortized, with periodic rehashing required on cycle detection or high load.

Chapter 14: Mostly Asked Important Questions – Part K

Q1. Describe the concept of "range kth order statistic" using a segment tree of order-statistic trees. How can you answer queries like "kth smallest in [L, R]"?

Answer: Build a segment tree where each node stores a balanced BST or order-statistic tree containing elements of that segment. For a query [L, R] and k, decompose [L,R] into O(log n) segments, then perform a binary search on value domain: at each mid-value, count how many numbers ≤ mid across these segments via order-statistic queries; adjust range until k-th smallest is found in O((log n)2)O((\log n)^2)O((logn)2).

Q2. Explain "compressed trie" for IP routing (Patricia trie) and how prefix matching is implemented efficiently.

Answer: A Patricia trie compresses chains of nodes with a single child by storing edge labels as bit strings. This reduces memory and traversal steps. For IP prefix matching, bits of the address are compared along edges until a leaf or mismatch—performing longest-prefix matching in O(length of key)O(\text{length of key})O(length of key).

Q3. What is a "2D segment tree"? Describe how it supports rectangle sum queries and updates in O((log n)2)O((\log n)^2)O((logn)2).

Answer: A 2D segment tree is a segment tree where each node itself contains another segment tree for the secondary dimension. A query or update in a rectangle region [x1,x2]×[y1,y2] traverses O(log n) primary nodes, each querying/updating its secondary segment tree in O(log n), resulting in O((log n)^2) time.

Q4. Explain the "Suffix Automaton" based solution for finding the number of occurrences of every substring in a string.

Answer: After constructing the suffix automaton with states and transitions, propagate counts from end states by topologically sorting states by length decreasing. Each state's occurrence count is the sum of counts of states that link to it. The number of occurrences of each substring equals the count in its corresponding end-state.

Q5. Describe "Fenwick Tree with range update and range query" using two BITs. How does it generalize prefix methods?

Answer: Use two BITs, BIT1 records slope changes, BIT2 records intercepts. To add v to [l, r], update BIT1[l] += v, BIT1[r+1] –= v; BIT2[l] += v*(l–1), BIT2[r+1] –= v*r. Query sum at x is sum(BIT1, x)*x – sum(BIT2, x). This generalizes range sum operations in O(log n).

Q6. Explain the concept of "persistent union-find" using rollback or path copying, and its use in offline connectivity queries.

Answer: To support historical finds/unions, maintain UF versions. In rollback, log changes to parent/rank stack and undo. With path-copying, duplicate only modified nodes. This supports dynamic connectivity queries like "connectivity at time t" offline in O(log n)O(\log n)O(logn) per operation with sort by time.

Q7. What is a "Combination of Mo's algorithm with updates"? Describe how time-dimension is added to Mo's pointer movement.

Answer: Mo's algorithm processes range queries offline. To handle updates, add a third dimension (time). Sort queries by block of L, then R, then time. Move pointers L, R, and apply or rollback updates as needed. Each move/update costs O(1), overall O((n + q)·n^{2/3}).

Q8. Describe the "Segment Tree Beats" technique for range chmin/chmax and maintain other aggregates efficiently.

Answer: Segment tree beats allow enforcing constraints like "max in range ≤ x" (chmin) while maintaining sums/min/max. Each node tracks first and second max values and their counts. If chmin value lies between them, apply it and update sum lazily; otherwise, push down. Each operation amortizes to O(log n).

Q9. Explain the concept of "Ht-Tree" (height-balanced tree) vs AVL and Red-Black trees. How are node heights maintained?

Answer: Ht-Tree is a height-balanced tree variant where each node stores its height. Upon insertion/deletion, if subtree heights differ >1, rotations rebalance and heights are updated. An Ht-Tree is similar to AVL but may have different rebalancing conditions (e.g. weight-based) while maintaining O(log n) height and operations.

Q10. Describe "Min-Max Segment Tree" that supports both range min and max queries simultaneously. How is it structured?

Answer: Each node stores two values: the minimum and maximum of its segment. Queries return both by combining child nodes: min = min(left.min, right.min), max = max(left.max, right.max). Updates propagate similarly. Each query/update runs in O(log n).

Chapter 15: Mostly Asked Important Questions – Part L

Q1. What is a "Wavelet Matrix"? Explain how it supports range counting, kth smallest, and predecessor queries in compressed memory.

Answer: A wavelet matrix is a variant of the wavelet tree optimized for large alphabets. It uses bit vectors per level to separate bits of values by significance. It supports range counting (number of elements ≤k in [L, R]), range kth smallest, and predecessor queries in O(log σ)O(\log \sigma)O(logσ) time, where σ\sigmaσ is the alphabet size, while using nlog σn \log \sigmanlogσ bits of space.

Q2. Describe the technique of "Local Search Trees" (LCT) for dynamic minimum spanning tree updates. How does it handle edge insertions and deletions efficiently?

Answer: LCT maintains the current MST and uses data structures like LCA to find replacement edges when the MST is updated. On edge deletion, it identifies the maximum edge on the cycle created and replaces it. Updates use link-cut or heavy-light structures to query maximum edges in O(log n)O(\log n)O(logn) time.

Q3. Explain "Range Mode Query" problem. How can it be solved with Mo's algorithm and frequency buckets?

Answer: Range Mode Query returns the most frequent value in [L,R]. Using Mo's algorithm to reorder queries, maintain frequencies and track current mode with buckets for counts. Updates and rollbacks adjust counts in O(1)O(1)O(1). Overall complexity is ~O((n+q)n)O((n + q)\sqrt{n})O((n+q)n).

Q4. What are "Rank-Select Dictionaries"? Provide an example of how they support constant-time bit retrieval and indexing.

Answer: Rank-select dictionaries support two operations on bitmaps: rank(b, i) = number of bits equal to b up to index i, and select(b, k) = position of kth b-bit. They achieve O(1)O(1)O(1) time using multi-level sampling (superblocks and blocks) and small lookup tables. They're foundational in compressed data structures like wavelet matrices.

Q5. Explain the "Divide-and-Conquer Optimization" technique in DP. How is it applied in problems with cost functions satisfying quadrangle inequality?

Answer: When DP transition costs satisfy quadrangle inequality, optimal partition indices follow monotonicity properties. Divide-and-conquer optimization recursively splits DP states, reducing overall complexity from O(n2)O(n^2)O(n2) to O(nlog n)O(n \log n)O(nlogn), using efficient queries for best partition points.

Q6. Describe "Histogram Stack Algorithm" for finding the largest rectangle in a histogram in O(n)O(n)O(n).

Answer: Traverse histogram bars, maintaining a stack of increasing heights. When a shorter bar appears, pop heights and compute area = height × width between current index and stack top. Continue until all bars processed. This yields maximal rectangle in one pass.

Q7. What is the "Minimum Enclosing Circle" problem? Explain the expected O(n)O(n)O(n)-time randomized algorithm for it.

Answer: The problem is finding the smallest circle enclosing all given points. A randomized incremental algorithm adds points one by one; if a point is outside the current circle, recompute the circle using at most 3 boundary points. Expected time is O(n)O(n)O(n).

Q8. Describe "Online Linear Regression" using stochastic gradient descent. How do data structures support incremental model updates?

Answer: Online linear regression updates parameters incrementally for each new data point: θ:=θ−η(xθ−y)x\theta := \theta - \eta (x\theta - y)xθ:=θ−η(xθ−y)x. Data structures like Fenwick trees or sliding window aggregates can support sum-of-squares or covariance computation efficiently for streaming data.

Q9. Explain the "Semi-Streaming Model" for graph computations. How are approximate matchings found in one pass with O(n)O(n)O(n) space?

Answer: In the semi-streaming model, edges arrive as a stream; space is limited to O(npolylog n)O(n \operatorname{polylog} n)O(npolylogn). Using greedy insertion and random sampling, one can approximate maximal matchings in a single pass by keeping a tentative matching and discarding conflicting edges, achieving a 2-approximation.

Q10. What is the "Combinatorial Heavy Hitters" problem? Explain how the Count-Min Sketch supports approximate counting with error guarantees.

Answer: Heavy hitters are items whose frequency exceeds a threshold. Count-Min Sketch uses multiple hash functions and an array of counters. On update, increment counters; on query, report the minimum counter among hashes. It provides an overestimate within additive error ϵn\epsilon nϵn and uses O(log (1/δ)/ϵ)O(\log(1/\delta)/\epsilon)O(log(1/δ)/ϵ) space to ensure probability of error < δ\deltaδ.

9 789369 917006

Printed at Repro India Ltd.